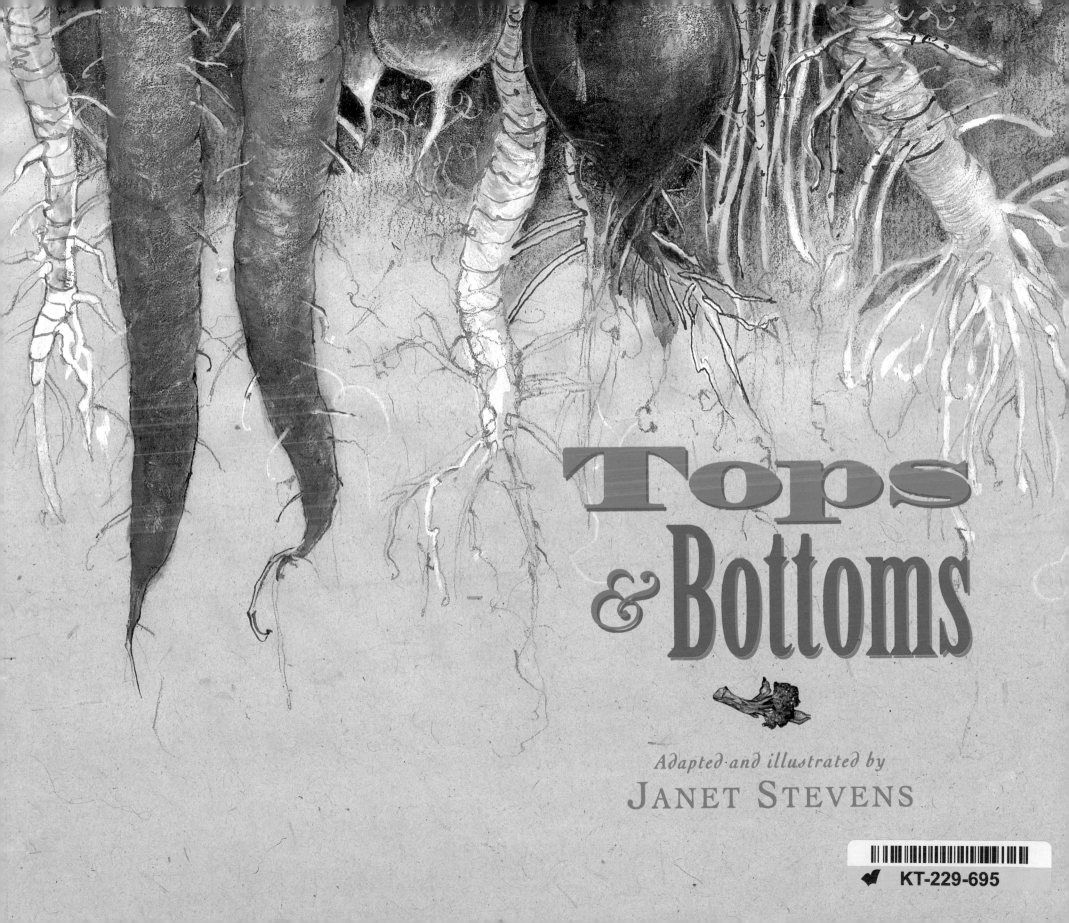

Tops
& Bottoms

Adapted and illustrated by

JANET STEVENS

For Judy Volc, who knows what kids like.

This edition published in 1997 by Hazar Publishing Ltd,
147 Chiswick High Road,
London, W4 2DT

First US edition published in 1995 by Harcourt Brace & Company

Copyright © Janet Stevens 1995

A catalogue record for this title is available from the British Library.

ISBN 1 874371 85 7 (Hardback)
ISBN 1 874371 87 3 (Paperback)

Printed and bound in Singapore.

ONCE upon a time there lived a very lazy bear who had lots of money and lots of land. His father had been a hard worker and a clever business bear, and he had given all of his wealth to his son.

But all Bear wanted to do was sleep.

Not far down the road lived a hare. Although Hare was clever, he sometimes got into trouble. He had once owned land, too, but now he had nothing. He had lost a risky bet with a tortoise and had sold all of his land to Bear to pay off the debt.

Hare and his family were not at all well off.

'The children are so hungry, Father Hare. We must think of something!' Mrs Hare cried one day. So Hare and Mrs Hare put their heads together and cooked up a plan.

The next day Hare hopped down the road to Bear's house. Bear, of course, was asleep.

'Hello, Bear, wake up! It's your neighbour, Hare, and I have an idea!'

Bear opened one eye and grunted.

'We can be business partners!' Hare said. 'All we need is this field right here in front of your house. I'll do the hard work of planting and harvesting, and we can split the profit right down the middle. Yes, sir, Bear, we're in this together. I'll work and you sleep.'

'Huh?' said Bear.

'So, what will it be, Bear?' asked Hare. 'The top half or the bottom half? It's up to you - tops or bottoms?'

'Well, let's see,' Bear said with a yawn. 'I'll take the top half, Hare. Yes, I'll take tops.'

Hare smiled. 'It's a done deal, Bear.'

So Bear went back to sleep, and Hare and his family went to work. Hare planted, Mrs Hare watered and everyone weeded.

Bear slept as the crops grew.

When it was time for the harvest, Hare called out, 'Wake up, Bear! You get the tops and I get the bottoms.'

Hare and his family dug up the carrots, the radishes and the beetroot. Hare plucked off all the tops, tossed them into a pile for Bear, and put the bottoms aside for himself.

Bear stared at his pile. 'But, Hare, all the best parts are in your half!'

'You chose the tops, Bear,' Hare said.

'Now, Hare, you've tricked me. You plant this field again - and this season I want the bottoms!'

Hare agreed. 'It's a done deal, Bear.'

So Bear went back to sleep, and Hare and his family
went to work. They planted, watered and weeded.

Bear slept as the crops grew.

When it was time for the harvest, Hare called
out, 'Wake up, Bear! You get the bottoms and I get
the tops.'

Hare and his family gathered up the lettuce, the broccoli and the celery. Hare pulled off the bottoms for Bear and put the tops in his own pile.

Bear looked at his pile and scowled. 'Hare, you have cheated me again.'

'But, Bear,' Hare said, 'you wanted the bottoms this time.'

Bear growled, 'You plant this field again, Hare. You've tricked me twice, and you owe me one season of both tops and bottoms!'

'You're right, poor old Bear,' sighed Hare. 'It's only fair that you get both tops and bottoms this time. It's a done deal, Bear.'

So Bear went back to sleep, and Hare and his family went to work. They planted, watered and weeded, then watered and weeded some more.

Bear slept as the crops grew.

When it was time for the harvest, Hare called out, 'Wake up, Bear! This time you get the tops *and* the bottoms!'

There in front of Bear's house lay a high field of sweetcorn. Hare and his family pulled up every cornstalk. Hare tugged off the roots at the bottom and the tassels at the top and put them in a pile for Bear. Then he carefully collected the ears of corn in the middle and placed them in his own pile.

Bear rubbed his eyes and watched.

'See, Bear? You get the tops and the bottoms. I get the middles. Yes, sir, Bear. It's a done deal!'

By now Bear was wide awake. 'That's it, Hare!' he yelled. 'From now on I'll plant my own crops and take the tops, bottoms and middles!'

Hare and his family scooped up the corn and hopped down the road towards home.

Bear never again slept through a season of planting and harvesting. Hare bought back his land with the profit from the crops, and he and Mrs Hare opened a vegetable stall.

And although Hare and Bear learned to live happily as neighbours, they never became business partners again!